What A Friend We Have In JESUS

By Harry Martin

Copyright © 1997 by Harry Martin
Orlando, Florida 32817

ALL RIGHTS RESERVED. No portion of this book may be reproduced in any form without the express written permission of the author.

Cover art by Andre LeBlanc, 27 E. 24th Street, Huntington Station, NY 11746-3701.

Printed in the United States of America

ISBN 0-9652205-2-4

What
A Friend
We Have In
JESUS

by Harry Martin

Harry Martin Publishing
Orlando, Florida, USA
407-207-4777

DEDICATION

This book is lovingly dedicated to the
memory of my father,
Harry Lewis Martin, Sr.
He is deeply missed
and fondly remembered.

Table Of Contents:

Introduction 6

What A Friend We Have In Jesus 10

Letting Go The Hand Of Jesus 14

Trusting In Jesus 25

Forsaken By Loved Ones 41

When Friends Despise Us 57

A Gift From Jesus 60

Satan Is A Liar 68

A Real Friend In Jesus 80

Just As We Are 91

Introduction

One of the greatest paradoxes in life is how often the most sin sick souls have the closest walk with Jesus. It is often the person who is the most scorned, rejected, and sinful who most realizes the depth and the breadth of the love of Jesus. It is most often the person whose life is racked with strife, trial and trouble who learn most about the love of Jesus.

Nevertheless, it is often when we are at our lowest point in life that we let go of Jesus' helping hand. Struggling Christians and non-Christians alike are often abandoned by Christians who are supposed to reflect the love of Jesus. In such cases, the struggling soul can easily assume Jesus has also abandoned them. After all, if those who claim to reflect the love of Jesus on earth will have nothing to do with us, why then would Jesus? Such thoughts often lead men and women who are having problems in their lives to let go the hand of Jesus at the very time they need Him the most.

Yet, Jesus never walks away from us no matter how troubled we are. No matter how lonely we feel, Jesus is always near. He never deserts us. He never leaves our side. Amazingly, the people who know these truths the best are those who have been brought to their knees by trials and suffering.

This book does one thing, and one thing only. Help every person who reads it realize what a friend we have in Jesus. To accomplish this purpose, I have related situations to the reader from my own life that helped me realize how much Jesus loves me. That is, after all, what Jesus has called all of us to do. Tell others what Jesus has done for us and how much He loves us all. Yet even more, to tell others there is nothing they can do, no depth to which they can fall, where Jesus is not with them.

Opening my heart and soul in this book has been hard to do. I would rather not have related some of these painful and embarrassing events from my life. It even occurred to me, if I wrote this book, there would be some who read it who will reject me as unworthy of their fellowship. Despite these fears I felt led by the Holy Spirit to give my testimony in this book to help encourage others who might be wondering if Jesus loves them.

My father always taught me you never knew who your real friends were until the going got tough. It is my hope my real friends will understand the purpose of revealing personal experiences in this book to help encourage others to trust Jesus.

In sharing these life experiences with the reader, I want to foster hope where there is despair. I want to foster joy where there is sorrow, new life where Satan has sown death and destruction. Some who read this book will complain I have been too blunt about people who abandoned me or deserted me when I needed them most. To these readers I will say this. To have blunted my testimony would have hindered my ability to help people better relate to Jesus.

These experiences illustrate how Jesus is a friend to even the most downtrodden soul. I have used my own experiences because others were not willing to have their personal experiences printed for the world to read. For most people such experiences are too personal, too painful to relate to others. Still, I know of no better witness than to tell others of what Jesus has done for me. This puts the love of Jesus in terms we can all understand.

Again, the purpose of this book is to tell others about how much Jesus loves us. We all know He does. Still, thousands of people who become discouraged and devastated by life forget Jesus loves them and is their friend too. I know of no better teacher than the life experiences of others. Since I am the author of this book, I use my life experiences. If Jesus will be my friend, He will be YOUR friend. If Jesus will be the friend of so chief a sinner as I, then Jesus will be anyone's friend.

Satan wants us to believe Jesus does not love us. I am here to tell the reader, in this book, Satan is a liar. However much a shambles your life is in, Jesus loves you. He is waiting for you to call His name and ask for His help and friendship this moment. We should never let anyone convince us we are beyond the love and friendship of Jesus.

What A Friend We Have In JESUS

I have a testimony I want to share. We may have never met, but we have a mutual friend, Jesus. I hope the reader will extend me the courtesy of reading this book and considering what I have to say.

I am a sinner. As a sinner I do not have one thing to recommend me to Jesus. Over my life many of my friends deserted me. My own brothers, a mother, a stepmother, a son all abandoned me to face the tribulations of life alone. Friend's I helped with jobs, loans, gifts of cars, money for medical bills and rent were not there for me when I needed them. The Court convicted me for a crime I committed in 1981. I have been falsely accused and punished for other crimes I did not commit. In 1993 I lost the only career that ever mattered to me, finding missing children through a missing children's charity I founded in 1990. While going blind not one person on my side of the family offered me one word of love, sympathy or hope. In fact, to this day not one brother, a sister, mother - not even my adult son will acknowledge my blindness. Enemies have tarnished and ruined my reputation. I have been left bankrupt and penniless. The church I had been raised in disfellowshipped me despite my pleas to remain so I would have their Christian love to help me survive tough times. My real mother committed suicide despite all my attempts to get her help and save her life. My father died without me even being able to get to his side to say goodbye. A dear nephew, Christopher Martin, died without me having the opportunity to go to his bedside to say goodbye. Throughout my childhood my father maintained to everyone I was learning disabled or mentally challenged.

The reason I relate these troubles to the reader at the beginning of this book is this. I know what it is like to be abandoned. I know what it is like to be rejected, misunderstood, falsely accused and wrongly punished. I know what it is like to be physically disabled in the prime of life. I do not want the reader to think he or she is reading a book written by someone who has never had a problem, or known trouble in their life. I have been in jail, I have been homeless, I have been outcast and forsaken. Still, Jesus, through his Holy Spirit always let me know He loved me and was there for me.

In the midst of my troubles and sorrows I learned the most important lesson of my entire life. That lesson is what a friend I have in Jesus and just how willing he is to bear all our sins and griefs. Amazingly, it is the very trials and tribulations I relate in this book which helped me understand what a friend Jesus is. How nothing on earth, or in heaven above, can remove me from the love of Jesus. Where Satan sought to destroy me, Jesus used his attempts to destroy as a means to help me realize my only hope was in His arms.

I believe with every fiber of my being this fundamental truth. Those who suffer the most in life hold the most promise as workers in the kingdom of God. Satan knows this truth and sets out to destroy these souls in any way he can. Satan has but one goal for each of us. He wants to bring us so low, so to ruin our lives, we can never be effective witnesses for Jesus or the Gospel. Nevertheless, it is when we hit bottom and rise again we become the most effective witnesses to the saving power of Jesus' grace.

King David committed murder. King Solomon became one of the greatest occult practitioners ever to live during his days of sinful living. Moses murdered an Egyptian in anger. Peter denied Jesus three times before the cock crowed, after they arrested Jesus. Paul was responsible for the deaths of hundreds of Christians before being converted. Yet, all these men have one thing in common. Despite their horrible sins, sometimes, capital crimes, each returned to Jesus and became powerful witnesses for the Lord.

Amazingly, Christians read the biblical accounts of these sins and crimes and marvel at how the Lord redeemed these fallen ones to Him. We glory in the biblical accounts of how a prostitute became a devoted follower of Jesus, how Jesus ate and partied with publicans and sinners to the point the Pharisees condemned him. Yet, today, in churches around the world Christians refuse to fellowship with sinners for fear of being tainted or brought low. Jesus, on the other hand, works with sinners today just as he did two thousand years ago. Jesus continues to be a friend to us all.

Letting Go The Hand Of Jesus

My first wife and I had divorced in 1972. Our only son, Jeremy, was placed in her custody because at the time the Courts nearly always gave the custody of children to the mother.

In 1976 my stepmother came to me and encouraged me to get custody of my son. His mother, in my stepmother's opinion, was not providing a good home environment for Jeremy. I went to court and got custody of Jeremy in December 1976. My stepmother immediately demanded I give custody of my son to her. I refused and my stepmother then encouraged my ex-wife to sue to get custody of my son back. If she won, they agreed my ex-wife would then give custody to my stepmother.

The custody battles lasted more than four years. I kept winning the cases while I kept my faith anchored in Jesus. Still, as the custody cases came and went I became very discouraged. Primarily because it was a Christian stepmother who was prodding my ex-wife to keep suing for custody. Case after case I watched as my Christian friends would not commit to helping me in court. Yet, my stepmothers' church friends went into court to testify for her. (We all attended the same church which made the strain even greater). I reasoned if I were unworthy of the support of my Christian friends in such an important matter I must be unworthy of Jesus' love too.

In 1981 I finally believed I was going to lose custody of my son due to lack of funds to continue paying my attorney. I began to panic as I realized I might only have a few more days to be with my son. If my ex-wife got custody she would turn my son over to my stepmother. I knew I would not get to see my son anymore. The anxiety I felt grew to an intolerable level. I began to reason Jesus must not love me if He could allow me to lose my son. This belief caused me to stop relying on Jesus for help in the upcoming custody hearing. The less I relied on Jesus the more my anxiety and panic grew.

The night before the hearing I sat at work about ready to have an emotional or mental breakdown. I was counting the money and preparing the night deposit for the Burger King where I worked. As I drove to the bank to put the deposit bag in the night depository my anxiety and panic grew unbearable. The more I thought about the possible loss of my son the next day the greater became my desperation to do something to keep him. Instead of praying to Jesus for strength and help, I took it upon myself to find a solution that guaranteed I would not lose my son. In a last ditch effort to escape the inevitable loss of my son the next day, I drove past the bank without making the deposit and went home.

It was now 2:00 in the morning. The court hearing was only eight hours away. I quickly packed a bag for my son and myself and loaded my little boy, still asleep, in my old Maverick and headed down I-20 toward Dallas, Texas. I will never forget the sheer panic and despair I felt as I drove out of Shreveport, Louisiana. I had no idea where we would go or how we would get there. In letting go of Jesus, I had let Satan triumph in my life.

As I drove the 190 miles from Shreveport to Dallas, I decided Jeremy and I would fly from Dallas to Seattle, Washington. At the time I was sure I could make the $7,900 deposit last long enough to get us an apartment, myself a job; and enroll Jeremy in a local school. I reasoned that since the two of us were together the theft of the deposit was justified. I had never committed a crime before and could not believe I had now. Still, an inner panic drove me to keep my son at all costs. At this point I was blinded to the fact my plan could not succeed.

My panic did not subside for two months. When it did, I realized what a horrible mistake I had made on that dark night in Shreveport, Louisiana. The Holy Spirit had been speaking to my heart the entire time. I just had not been listening. Now the voice of the Holy Spirit came through loud and clear and I at last heard his tender voice. The Holy Spirit pleaded with me to stop the course I was on right then. He convinced me that a life of crime was not a life Jesus wanted me, or my son, to live. The counsel of the Holy Spirit was clear. Return home to Shreveport and turn myself in to police.

I will never forget the heart wrenching tears which flowed from my heart that night in Seattle. I knew I had made a terrible mistake. I knew that if I returned my son to his mother, or to his grandparents, pending the outcome of my situation I would probably never see him again.

I imagined I would spend years in prison. I knew my stepmother would use this episode to prejudice my son against me as he grew up. Everything I had done had played right into Satan's plan.

I spent hours that night praying for some other course of action, but, none was forthcoming. The command of the Holy Spirit was simple and clear. Return to Shreveport, admit what I had done, and do everything in my power to make my wrong right. I began to realize how David felt when he realized his terrible sin in having another woman's husband killed so he could have her for himself. Did David not realize at some point in the commission of this terrible sin what the consequences would be? Or, did he, like me, simply not listen to the pleadings of the Holy Spirit? Whatever the case I knew I had to do what the Holy Spirit was telling me to do if I ever wanted to get past this situation.

The next morning I called my closest friend in Shreveport, Louisiana. I asked him to call my attorney and make arrangements for me to return with Jeremy to Shreveport and turn myself in. My friend promised he would do so and then call me back that night with the details.

Well, my friend did call me back that night with the details. Instead of making arrangements with an attorney he had called the police and turned me in. He told me he was sorry to have spoiled my chance to turn myself in. Still, he felt if I got away at once I had a chance to get to Shreveport and turn myself into police. Whatever I did had to be quick because Seattle police were probably on their way to my house to arrest me even as we were speaking.

The news shattered me. Turning myself in was important to me. I wanted everyone to know I was sorry for what I had done wrong. If the police got to arrest me before I had the chance to turn myself in no one would believe I was sorry for what I had done. Since the only transportation I had was a Honda 250 Twin-Star motorcycle I knew there was very little I could take that night except myself, my son and some blankets.

I did not want my son having to ride from Seattle to Shreveport, a distance of more than two thousand miles, on a motorcycle. Even worse, it was the middle of February. That meant much of the distance I was going to travel would be in snow and bitter cold. To guarantee my son's safety I took him and a puppy I had bought him to Sea-Tac Airport and put them on an airplane to Shreveport. I then called my father to let him know he would need to pick my son up at the airport. Knowing my son was safe I retreated to a section of woods next to the airport to await the morning light.

I will never forget how I watched the jets pass over me in the night as they took off for their various destinations. I knew one carried my precious son and wondered when, if ever, I would get to see him again. As I fell off to a very disturbed sleep, I asked Jesus to help me succeed in carrying out the unction of the Holy Spirit.

As I began my trip the next morning, I was not sure I would even get out of town. I found out later that within minutes of my leaving the house the night before the police had shown up in force to take me into custody. Still, I did make my escape. For the next week I traveled on my little motorcycle through mountain passes that were bitter cold. I traversed deserts with winds so fierce they nearly blew me over. I rode through nights so long I thought the sun would never rise again. Nevertheless, thanks to Jesus' watch care I made it to Shreveport.

To sum up, I did succeed in turning myself into police. Despite my lawyer trying to convince me to plead not guilty I kept my promise to the Holy Spirit and pled guilty. The Court was merciful enough to give me the opportunity to repay the money I had stolen. The Court also adjudicated me as a convicted felon and ordered me to serve five years probation.

Every fear I had about my stepmothers' getting custody of my son came true. My stepmother denied me visitations, refused me holidays with my son. I never again got to enjoy the close relationship my son and I had while I had custody of him.

Praise Jesus, I did repay every dime I had stolen. It took me seven years instead of five. Still, the Court worked with me and with the strength provided by Jesus I successfully served my term of probation.

Again, the point of this story is to let others who are going through similar circumstances know how much Jesus loves us all. There is nothing we can do which will separate us from the love and friendship of Jesus. We cannot judge how much Jesus loves us by how other people treat us. After the Court adjudicated me in this case, the church I had grown up in disfellowshipped me. This church did not want convicted felons like me as members of their congregation.

I will never forget the day I was called to a church meeting by a few of the church elders. Coincidentally, the very church elders who had joined with my stepmother in her custody cases against me. I pleaded with these men to allow me to remain in their fellowship. I knew the Holy Spirit had impressed me such fellowship would be critical to my success in making my wrong right. Not withstanding my pleas, the church elders asked me to leave and never return.

This is why I make the point we cannot depend on how our friends, relatives, or even our church treats us when we make mistakes. The important point is that Jesus loves us and is our friend. Jesus never deserts us, abandons us, disowns us, or turns His face from us. No matter how much we resist His love He continues to try to draw us to Him. There is no crime we can commit, no depth to which we can fall, where Jesus is not there waiting for us to call His name and accept His friendship. It is regrettable when we as imperfect men and women do commit crimes or fall so low our lives are left in a shambles. Jesus does not want us to fall at all. Yet, when we do, He is still our friend. All we need do is call upon His holy name and ask for his friendship and help and He is there for us.

Dear Friend, Jesus is ready and willing to bear all our sins and griefs. I hope the reader has never committed a crime like I did. Still, even if the reader has, Jesus is there for you. Do not misunderstand me, the Holy Spirit made it clear to me I had to do whatever it took to make my wrong right. Which in my case meant turning myself in. Admitting I had committed a crime was important. As was asking for an opportunity to repay the money I had stolen. Finally, it was important I abide by any sentence or punishment the Court imposed on me. Trusting the Holy Spirit did not absolve me of my responsibility to do the right thing. Still, the Holy Spirit promised He would be with me throughout the ordeal. He kept His promise.

The fact Jesus was my friend no matter what did not relieve me of my responsibility to make my wrong right either. Still, Jesus made it clear he would be with me as I struggled to do the right thing.

The Holy Spirit and Jesus will do the same thing for anyone. Whatever we may have done wrong in our life, Jesus, through the Holy Spirit, will help us. We will not escape punishment. Nevertheless, the Holy Spirit and Jesus will be with us every moment. Best of all, we will have the satisfaction of knowing we finally did the right thing.

Trusting In Jesus

We can always trust in Jesus. If you are a teenager with a problem, an adult facing a crisis, or a discouraged soul ready to quit, you can take it to Jesus in prayer. No one needs to call on a psychic to find out what to do with a problem. Psychics' are Satan's substitute for prayer. The reader need not confide in friends who will spread his or her problem through gossip and cause embarrassment and heartache. Instead, you can take everything to God in prayer.

One of the biggest problems I have always had with formal Christianity is how often the very people who should encourage a sinner the most, do the least. Indeed, many Christians will turn their noses up at a fellow Christian in distress. They think they are too good to allow themselves to be tainted by a struggling friend. In Jesus day a sect called Pharisee's were notorious for this attitude. In their eyes, their righteousness, their own works, was their ticket to Heaven. They did not mind standing in the public square to loudly proclaim their prayers extolling their own good works for all to hear. Pharisees' were not interested in encouraging others in the love of Jesus. Indeed, the Pharisees were afraid that associating with sinners would taint them. To keep from being tainted by association with sinners, Pharisees kept a safe distance. Keeping this distance also kept the Pharisees from being an effective witness to sinners about the love of Jesus. Jesus detested the Pharisee's for this reason. In fact, after one encounter with a group of Pharisees Jesus had this to say. "...Verily I say unto you, That the publicans and harlots go into the Kingdom of God before you." Matthew 21:31.

Still, no matter how supposed Christians treat us, we can always go directly to Jesus in prayer. No matter how far from God we may be, when we pray in Jesus Name, we are only a word away from the love and help only Jesus can offer us.

More important, we can offer a prayer to Jesus no matter where we are. Are you alone at home without a friend? Jesus is only a prayer away. Are you in a hospital bed dying of cancer? Jesus is only a prayer away. Are you in a prison cell awaiting trial for a crime you did, or did not commit? Jesus is only a prayer away. Have you just become disabled and found that no one in your family will have anything to do with you anymore? Jesus is only a prayer away. Have you lost your job, your home, your future? Jesus is only a prayer away. How unfortunate when we do not take advantage of the privilege to carry everything to God in prayer.

You see, dear reader, prayer is nothing more than having a talk with Jesus. Prayer is when we tell Jesus what is on our mind. He wants to hear what is on our minds. Prayer is not a vain repetition of words we recite dozens of times. Prayer is not some holy exercise we can only engage in at church. Prayer is simply our having a conversation with Jesus.

Let me share something I have learned about prayer. I make most of my mistakes in life when I do not pray. When I engage in prayer with Jesus, I make fewer mistakes. We are all human, and we all sin. Still, when I have a prayer relationship with Jesus, I find I make a lot fewer mistakes in life.

This means it is important for all of us to have a prayer relationship with Jesus. Even those who pride themselves on being better than everyone else need a prayer relationship with Jesus. If for no other reason than to ask for humility in dealing with others.

I would invite the reader, no matter where you are right now, to begin a prayer relationship with Jesus. Wherever you are right now, offer up a prayer to Jesus and thank Him for being there for you, for being your friend. Ask Jesus to help you understand what to do with whatever problem or situation is affecting you right now. Having a problem doing this? Well, maybe an experience I had in 1993 will help the reader understand just how easy it is to pray to Jesus and how much He wants to help you. This example will also help the reader see what can happen when one does NOT go to Jesus in prayer.

In 1993 two children in trouble falsely accused me of committing a crime. I knew I had not committed this heinous crime. Still, the police had no way of knowing whether I had committed this crime or not. I was arrested in my office on March 23, 1993. It is a day I will never forget. I was the lead news story for weeks to come in all the local media.

The worst part of this whole experience was the fact I had let my prayer relationship with

Jesus fall by the wayside. I had stopped attending church due to work demands. The net result of all of this was I felt myself unworthy to rely on Jesus in this crisis. I believed Satan's lie that since I had not been attending church, Jesus would not hear my pleas for help.

To sum up, I took a plea bargain in September 1993. I was innocent. Still, I was in the process of going blind and did not want to go blind in a prison cell. I knew juries frequently convicted innocent people accused of what the two children had accused me of, lewd and lascivious conduct with a child. The people who had worked for me at America's Missing Children could have testified on my behalf. They knew I had devoted my life to locating missing children, not molesting them. These people abandoned me, knowing that if the jury wrongly convicted and sent me to prison they would inherit the charity I had founded. So, instead of helping me, these so-called friends did just that, abandoned me.

Friendless, falsely accused and going blind I got discouraged and accepted a plea bargain. This guaranteed me I would not do time in prison or get wrongly convicted by a jury afraid to acquit someone accused of molesting children. Taking a plea bargain knowing I was innocent was the worst mistake I have ever made in my entire life. I had to serve two years of house arrest and five years of probation. I was also branded a sexual offender for the rest of my life even though a jury did not convict me because I took a plea bargain. Amazingly, in a short newspaper story that appeared in the paper the next day, the prosecuting attorney admitted she had a shaky case because the children's stories kept changing. When I read the depositions of the two children who had accused me I was astounded. One child would testify I did something to the other child. The police would then ask the other child if this allegation were true. The other child would often testify that no such incident occurred. In fact, in some parts of the deposition the children had admitted they had made up most, if not all, of their allegations. Unfortunately, I was not aware of much of this information until after I had taken the plea bargain.

  I did go blind during this period, and America's Missing Children did fall into the hands of my co-workers. They mismanaged the agency so badly the State later ordered it closed because the husband and wife who took it over were no longer finding any missing children. Instead, they were using the money to buy cars, take vacations, and enrich themselves. If I had trusted Jesus to help me in this crisis I might have saved not only myself from ruin. I might have saved a successful missing child agency too.

During my first year of house arrest, I often wondered how I could have let my prayer relationship with Jesus go at the very time I needed it the most? I was about to get another chance to learn a lesson in trusting in Jesus. Jesus often allows misfortune and trial to befall us over and over again until we do learn the lesson He wants us to learn. He was about to allow me to be tried in the fire again.

One problem in taking a plea bargain in any case is that you automatically set yourself up for anyone else who wants to come along and falsely accuse you of another crime. Since you have already plea bargained to one crime, there is always another person who expects they can use you as a scapegoat hoping you will do the same thing again.

In September 1994 I got a disturbing phone call from my brother who lived in Kissimmee,

Florida. He had just lost his oldest son four months earlier to muscular dystrophy. The death of my nephew had also been very hard on me because he and I had enjoyed a good relationship. I was disabled, and so was my nephew. I was blind. He had muscular dystrophy. This gave us a common bond. So, I took his death very hard, too. His death also helped me realize how short life could be and I set out to develop an even stronger relationship with my brother. So, when he called in September 1994 I was glad to hear from him.

His call shattered any hope I had we could ever have that closer relationship. His surviving son had always been troubled. This was due in large part to the fact my brother had to devote a large amount of his time to his oldest son who was suffering from muscular dystrophy. To get his share of attention from his father my youngest nephew would often act out. He had missed months of school the year before. The boy would be gone the entire day without his father ever checking to see where he was or what he was doing. It turned out, after my oldest nephews' death, that my surviving nephew had gotten involved in stealing, drugs and sexual activity. This resulted in his finally being sent to a Charter Forest facility in Kissimmee for treatment and counseling.

In the course of his treatment he had to attend group therapy sessions and tell everyone anything that might be bothering him. A few weeks before he went into Charter Forest he had visited his grandmother, my stepmother, in Waskom, Texas. While there, he related how a number of people in his community had forced him to do drugs, steal, and engage in illicit sexual activity with other adults. My brother and I had discussed these revelations by my nephew several times in the last few weeks. I figured this was the subject of this phone call from my brother. Especially when he asked me if I had any idea what had happened to my nephew again.

We had already discussed all of this in a previous phone call a few days earlier. So, I told my brother that I did NOT know what else had happened to my nephew. My brother insisted I most certainly did know and he wanted me to tell him. I told my brother that, except for what I had already heard about, I did not know of anything new that might have happened to his youngest son. Then my brother hit me with the devastating blockbuster. In his group therapy session at Charter Forest the counselors asked that my nephew reveal to the group something bothering him. Under pressure to reveal the source of his continued distress my nephew informed the group that I had molested him since he was seven years old until the age of twelve. My brother went on to inform me that everyone believed him because he had no reason to lie.

As part of his therapy the staff told him he had to call someone and tell them about my abuse of him. He chose to call his grandmother, my stepmother. The same grandmother he had just visited a few weeks earlier and to whom he had told the tales of how people in his community had abused and hurt him. Amazingly, without ever once mentioning me as an abuser. That despite the fact my stepmother would have believed anything of which he might have accused me.

I told my brother I had never abused his son. I could not understand why he would implicate me along with the dozen or so other people he had accused. My brother did not accept this. He demanded I confess saying I owed it to him to do so. My head was spinning and I was in shock. How could my own brother believe I would molest his son? Finally, I told my brother I did not owe it to him to confess to something I had not done and ended the conversation. One thing was clear to me. Satan knew how important my relationship with my brother was in surviving my house arrest and probation. I was certain this was Satan's way of preventing my brother from being there for me in this crisis. Or, for me being there for my brother if he ever needed me in the future.

I needed Jesus and I knew it. There was no doubt my nephew was using me as a scapegoat for some reason. I was certain I knew the reason. Still, I knew my brother would never give any credence to what I thought the problem was. Satan was definitely going too succeed in his plan to cost me yet another friend, my brother, if he could.

My hopes were shattered. I was halfway through my two-year house arrest for a crime I did not commit. Now my nephew was accusing me of another crime which he knew I had not committed. My fear was this new allegation would result in my immediate arrest and incarceration.

I began to pray to Jesus in earnest. I had lost my brother. I knew that. I had no close friends due to the allegations the year before and because of my present situation. Frankly, I had no one to turn to but Jesus. Ironically, it had been only one year ago when I did not rely on Jesus to help me. Was I getting a second chance to learn to rely on Jesus, I wondered? It seemed I was. I did not think Jesus was the one causing this to happen to me. Satan is the father of lies, and I knew Satan was the one who was responsible for these false allegations. Still, Jesus can make bad things work together for good to them that love the Lord. It was my hope Jesus would help overrule Satan's purpose in this matter. I intended to ask Jesus to do just that.

One month after this phone call I heard a knock on the door. I had prayed fervently since my brother's phone call Jesus would overrule my nephew's false allegations and help me remain free of any further arrests, prosecutions or plea bargains. Still, I did not know if this was the police coming to arrest me, or a friend coming to visit.

When I opened the door, I asked who was

there. Since I was now blind, I had no way of knowing whom I was facing. It was my probation officer and a HRS Investigator. The two had come to ask me about my nephew's allegations. For the next hour HRS talked to me and got my side of the story. I told HRS I felt my nephew was troubled about the fact he and his older brother had engaged in sexual activity together. My nephew had once confided in me he was afraid that because he helped his crippled brother masturbate might mean he was homosexual. I had assured my nephew this would not make him gay, nor did it mean he was gay. That he should speak with his father or a counselor about the matter.

I told the HRS representative I felt counselors at Charter Forest could see something was still bothering him. When they pressured him to tell them what was still bothering him he chose to make up allegations about me. This was easier than admitting to a group of teenagers in a group therapy session he had sex with his brother. Accusing me spared him the embarrassment of admitting the truth to the other young people in his group. His allegations also took the focus off his own wrongdoings. By accusing others of molesting him, my youngest nephew became a victim instead of a perpetrator. He now had an excuse for all his own wrongdoing. The ploy had worked.

I also told the HRS worker I found it ironic that only a few month's prior my nephew had been visiting my stepmother, his grandmother. Yet, he said nothing about me abusing him to her. He knew she would believe anything he said to her about me. Yet, knowing that, he still did not make a single allegation about me to her at the time. I maintained to the HRS lady the reason he did not tell his grandmother I had abused him then was because he knew I had not. Only later, while under pressure to reveal something bothering him in a group therapy session, did he finally make up allegations about me.

When the HRS case worker had finished listening to me she made two comments which left me hoping Jesus was intervening on my behalf. First, she commented that it was clear to her I had not even had contact with my nephew over many of the time periods he alleged I had abused him. Second, she stated it was common for young people to make up stories in group therapy sessions. This helped them avoid telling the group about something they might have done which would embarrass them. In my nephew's case this would have been the sexual activity with his brother. By accusing me of sexually abusing him, my nephew took all the focus off what was really bothering him and focused the counselors attention on me.

After HRS left, I prayed Jesus would overrule this matter so that Satan would not succeed in his attempt to further destroy me with these allegations. I could not understand why Satan was so intent on destroying me so utterly I could never show my face in my community again. Still, I knew he would succeed unless Jesus saw fit to answer my prayer and overrule this matter.

Now, let me make a point here. I do not presume to know what Jesus' plans to allow to happen to me, or to anyone else. Even if I had been arrested and incarcerated it would not have meant Jesus had abandoned me. Remember, innocent people are falsely accused and wrongly convicted every day. One only need read the Old Testament story of Joseph to see an example of how God allows innocent people to go to prison and serve time for crimes they did not commit.

So, I did not know whether Jesus would overrule this situation or not. I hoped he would, I prayed he would. Still, whatever happened I knew I needed to trust Jesus.

Two and a half years passed without any further word about this matter coming to me. I began to trust Jesus had answered my prayers to help me by overruling the situation of these latest false allegations. In 1993 I had not trusted in Him, in 1994 I did. It was my hope these allegations would never raise their ugly head again. Nevertheless, two and a half years after my nephew initially made the false allegations the matter did raise its ugly head again. I would now develop an even deeper relationship with Jesus.

Forsaken By Loved Ones

My son and I had not been on good terms with each other since I had missed his college graduation in May 1993. This was the time I was battling the original false allegations of lewd and lascivious conduct with a child. As the reader will recall, these allegations surfaced in March 1993. The Court had enjoined me not to leave the State of Florida while the matter was pending in Court. As a result, I could not attend my son's graduation in Keene, Texas. I had hoped he would understand the extenuating circumstances, but he did not.

From May 1993 when I missed his graduation until the Fall of 1997, I tried many times to get in touch with my son with no success. I wrote him letters, sent him cards and presents on his birthday and at Christmas. Still, he never acknowledged any of my attempts to contact him. When he came to my nephews funeral in April 1994 he refused to speak with me, or have any contact with me at all. I was not even sure he was receiving any of my letters or gifts since I did not know if I had his correct address. I knew my stepmother had his address. So, I wrote her a letter and asked her to give it to me. This way I would be sure he was getting my mail and presents. She refused. This left me with no sure way to confirm my son's address.

One day in September 1997 I heard my fax machine go off. Since I normally did not get faxes on Saturday morning, I was anxious to see who would be trying to reach me via a fax. To my surprise it was a fax from my sister who was in Nashville, Tennessee for an Amway convention at the time. The fax alerted me I would be getting a land deed in the mail in a day or two. She went on to say it was critical I signed this land deed the day I received it and overnighted it back to the land deed office in Carthage, Texas. As it turned out, my stepmother was selling land which was left to her and the other children when my father died. By law the only way my stepmother could sell the land was if all the children signed the deed authorizing its sale. My sister ended her fax saying she loved me. This was the first time I had heard from my sister since my nephew had died in April 1994.

The paperwork did arrive as my sister had

said it would. As I reviewed the paperwork, it occurred to me this was the perfect opportunity to get my son's address from either my stepmother, or my sister. After all, they were asking me to sign away rights to my portion of land my father had left me. If I were willing to sign the deed and allow my stepmother and sister to sell the land, I hoped they would be willing to return the favor by giving me my son's address. My stepmother still refused to give it to me. I was flabbergasted she refused because she had so much to lose. If I did not sign the deed, my stepmother and sister could not sell the land. My stepmother and sister needed the deed signed and back at the land deed office by the following Monday. Both needed to close the sale of their respective houses by then. Without my signature they could not close the sale of their houses, and it would take a court hearing to settle the dispute. Yet, this had been the way matters were always settled in my family. You do what we want you to do without our giving any courtesies in return; or, you pay a price.

    I refused to sign the land deed on the basis my stepmother and sister would not extend me the courtesy of giving me my son's address. That night, for the first time in seven years, I got a phone call from my son. He was furious I would not sign the land deed. We talked for an hour or so and agreed. He would give me his address despite not wanting to do so. He also agreed to meet with me the end of February, some five months in the future. In return I would sign the land deed. Based on his word I signed the land deed and overnighted it to the land deed office in Carthage, Texas. Based on my conversation with my son I was certain the fact I signed the deed would give me a chance at least to talk about our relationship as father and son. In fact, he had told me, by signing the land deed, I would impress him enough to do just that. We would talk about our relationship and meet together the end of February.

Once I signed the land deed and delivered it, I found my son had duped me. I had found my son's E-mail address on the Internet service we both used. Since he knew I would be communicating with him about our upcoming meeting in February I emailed him several messages meant to help work out the details of our visit. Each and every E-mail message was deleted without being read. I tried sending him several letters to work out the details of our meeting, they were never answered. The horrible truth dawned on me that my son had lied to me. He had never intended to meet with me or talk to me. His only goal had been to get me to sign the land deed. Having accomplished that he cut me off. In 1994, Satan had helped destroy any hope I had of developing a stronger relationship with my brother. Now, two years later, Satan was shattering any hope I had of building a stronger relationship with my son. Satan was intent on depriving me of the love and friendship of my entire family.

The reader might wonder how any of this relates to my nephew's false allegations raising their ugly head again in 1997. The matter of the land deed had everything to do with these allegations raising their head again in 1997.

When my son and I spoke on the phone that night about the land deal, he made it clear he was very angry about how I felt about my stepmother. He stated he felt I needed to be put in my place and taught a lesson. I attempted to explain to him my feelings for my stepmother. That they were based on her more than thirty years of mental and emotional abuse of me. My explanations fell on deaf ears. All he knew was he wanted me to be punished in some way for refusing to sign the land deed. The fact I finally did apparently did not matter to him. This is another trait of my family. It does not matter if you ultimately do what they consider to be the right thing. It only matters you did what they considered the wrong thing initially. The fact I finally did sign the land deed would have meant very little to my family. It is this attitude by my family which colored my view on how Jesus deals with us for so many years. Because most of my family consider themselves to be good Christians, I reasoned they were reflecting how Jesus deals with us. In other words, if we did the wrong thing initially, it does not matter to Jesus if we later do the right thing. Still, the Burger King situation taught me this was not true.

    I was sitting at home on March 7, 1997 listening to television when I heard a knock at the door. When I answered the door two men identified themselves as Orlando Police Detectives and stated they wanted to speak to me about a matter regarding my nephew. I immediately knew the allegations made by my nephew in 1994 had surfaced again. I never dreamed I was going to hear what I did when I invited them in to talk to me about the matter. Once inside, the detectives explained to me they had gotten a call in January 1997 with further information about the allegations my nephew had made.

As it turned out, my son had called the police and told them he had seen me abuse two stepdaughters from a previous marriage in 1985. My son would have been fourteen at the time. The reason his age is important is if he had seen such abuse then he was old enough to report it then. He did not have to wait twelve years to report any such abuse he had witnessed. In fact, he was in the custody of my stepmother in 1985. He was attending a Christian school. Had my son told *anyone* he had seen such abuse in 1985 my stepmother would have believed him and helped him report the allegations to the police.

The police went on to explain since my own son was willing to cooperate in the investigation of my nephews 1994 allegations they had reopened the case for further review. I cannot tell the reader the immensity of the shock I felt as I sat with those two detectives. My own son, now twenty-six years old, had joined my nephew in making false allegations against me.

I went on to explain to the detectives how I found it strange my son had not come forward with these allegations in 1993. He knew then I was being accused of lewd and lascivious conduct with children. He had every opportunity to come forward then. More importantly, he had every opportunity to come forward in 1994 when my nephew had falsely accused me of molesting him. The detectives answered they could not explain the failure of my son to come forward at either of those times with his information. When the detectives left they informed me they would turn over the matter to the State Attorney General's office. It would then be up to that office whether or not I would be charged, arrested, and tried on the allegations my nephew had made against me in 1994.

I simply could not understand how God could allow me to go through all of this again. I went through it in 1993, again in 1994, and now it was happening to me again in 1997. Still, I knew I had to trust in Jesus, just as I had in 1994.

The emotional weight of this crisis was so crushing there was no way I could handle it without Jesus. So, I did exactly what I had done in 1994. I went to Jesus and asked for help. I did not presume Jesus would make the problem miraculously disappear overnight. I did not presume Jesus would spare me an arrest, or trial, or imprisonment. I just knew that whatever happened, however the matter proceeded, I would need Jesus' help to help me get through it.

I did feel led by the Holy Spirit to get an attorney this time. The problem was I did not have the twenty or thirty thousand dollars most attorneys want to handle such a case. Without some help from Jesus I would never be able to afford an attorney. After praying about the matter I felt led by the Holy Spirit to write three letters to three different attorneys in Orlando, Florida. The point of the letters was to find an attorney who would represent me for a fee I could afford. More importantly, one who would begin to represent me even before any charges were filed. This way, if I did get arrested, I would already have an attorney to represent me.

Within days one of these letters got me a consultation with Hennigan & Malone, a law firm in Orlando. I explained the matter to them and asked for their help. The firm agreed to charge me a fee which I found I could afford, and which was much less than I had expected. It was still a large fee, but it was a fee I could manage to pay. When I left the offices of Hennigan & Malone that morning I had legal representation. In my opinion, the Lord had miraculously intervened on my behalf to see I had competent legal representation in this matter.

I was now left with the matter of how to get through each day. I did not know whether I would be charged and arrested a second time for crimes I had not committed. In the flesh I could not imagine not getting arrested. After all, this was my own son willing to claim he had seen me molest a little girl in 1985. In the Spirit I was trusting Jesus to work His will in this matter. March turned into April, and April turned into May. I did not hear a word from the police or from my attorney. I continued to pay my legal fee the first of every month. Most of all, I continued to pray to Jesus for His help and mercy in this matter.

It was my contention my son was making the allegation to make good on his threat to make me pay for not signing the land deed back in September. As I have already stated, in my family it never mattered if you eventually did the right thing. If you did the wrong thing initially, or what my family considered being the wrong thing initially, what you did later would not make any difference. Since my son had been raised by my stepmother, she had given him her set of values. It did not matter to him I finally did sign the land deed and do what they considered the right thing. It only mattered to him I initially did the wrong thing. Since my son had never before alleged I had molested anyone, I found it very telling he would make such allegations now. Since he and I had been on bad terms for many years, he had no reason to withhold any such information for twelve years. It was clear to me these allegations on his part were his way of getting his revenge against me for my bad relationship with my stepmother. Especially since such heinous allegations usually result in the arrest and conviction of the accused. Even when there is no evidence to support the allegations. Even if the police never arrest the accused, such allegations usually result in the loss of reputation and friends.

Accusing people of molesting children provides an easy way for malicious people to take out their revenge on anyone they have a grudge against. Especially since everyone usually believes such allegations. A fact which often results in the total ruin of the life of the person being accused. Still, as the months passed while the legal system decided what to do with the allegations, I drew closer and closer to Jesus. He was my only hope whatever finally happened.

If the allegations resulted in my arrest and imprisonment pending trial, I knew a close relationship with Jesus would be essential to maintain my sanity. If the State filed the charges and the police arrested me, I knew the media would broadcast my dilemma all over Central Florida. The effect of this would be to alienate my neighbors against me. I was certain my friends at church would be hard pressed to know how to react to such news. I also knew persons accused of such crimes were often evicted from their apartments. I knew this would leave my wife and me in dire circumstances.

If they charged and arrested me I knew I would lose my guide dog, Frankie. Since my wife was still recovering from a serious car accident there was no way she could take care of my guide dog if I were in jail. Even if I got bonded out of jail, pending a trial, the Court would most likely hold me on house arrest. This would prevent me from taking my guide dog on his daily exercise walks or out for his restroom breaks. I would lose my main source of mobility as a blind person. More important, I would lose a wonderful friend and companion, my guide dog. These are just a few of the problems I had to ponder while the State made a decision on whether or not to file charges.

In an effort to help my church family cope with the shock of me being arrested and charged with such a crime, I called my Pastor, Dr. Dean Chapman. He came over to my home and I explained the entire situation to him. I knew, if I were arrested, the Pastor would be the first to get phone calls from fellow members trying to find out what was going on. Not being forewarned would be unfair for him.

In explaining to Dr. Chapman the events of 1993 and 1994, I also gave him an option. I told my Pastor if he were not comfortable with having someone with my problems as a member of the congregation I would stop coming. My experience of being disfellowshipped from the church I had grown up in still haunted me. Much to the credit of Dr. Chapman, he assured me I was welcome at Westminster Presbyterian Church despite my past or present problems. He understood perfectly the church was a place for sinners to fellowship and come to know Jesus.

I also knew there was the possibility a jury might wrongly convict me if the charges were filed. A conviction on these charges could send me to prison for the rest of my life. I would lose the companionship of my wife, my church friends, my guide dog. I would lose everything and spend the rest of my life in a prison. Joseph was falsely accused, wrongly convicted and unfairly imprisoned by Pharaoh when Potiphar's wife claimed he raped her. God did not spare Joseph years in prison. God did work the situation to Joseph's good and His glory. If the Lord could allow this fate to befall Joseph, I did not want to presume I could not go to prison on false charges too. If I did, it seemed my life would be over.

There was another possibility though. The same outcome which occurred in 1994 could happen again. The allegations could be recognized for what they were, false. Instead of the charges being filed, the matter could be overruled by Jesus. I would survive another Satanic attempt to ruin my life. My wife and I would be able to remain together, and I would not lose my faithful guide dog, Frankie.

I remember joking to my wife one day in May 1997 as I was working to complete this book. Not yet knowing how this situation was going to work out I told her she might have to be the one who finished this book. I might be the first person to get a copy in prison. The irony that the author of a book of this kind might be the first one to receive a copy of it in prison for encouragement was not lost on either of us.

What was the final outcome of the 1994 allegations being reinvestigated in 1997? I finally got a phone call from my lawyer telling me the State of Florida had decided not to file charges against me. The State could not find any reason to believe I had ever molested my nephew and so had dropped the matter. Satan was defeated in his plan to see me imprisoned for a crime I did not commit.

When Friends Despise Us

We have all lost friends to disagreements or misunderstandings. Many of us have had some friends despise and forsake us when bad things happen to us. If the reader has never had a friend, or a loved one, despise or forsake them they are fortunate. How wonderful it is to know Jesus sticks with us even when some or all our friends despise and forsake us.

Earlier in this book I mentioned how, when in 1993 I was falsely accused of a crime, the very people who could have helped me the most were the people who abandoned me to the situation. As I said, these people had more to gain by abandoning me than by helping me in my crisis. Helping me would leave me in control of the charity I had founded. Abandoning me to the situation left me in a position where I could become discouraged and give up the fight to prove my innocence. Or even worse, be wrongly convicted of a crime I did not commit. The irony is, Jesus knows exactly how it feels to be in this situation. The night Jesus was arrested even his most ardent follower, Peter, denied him three times.

This is the reason Jesus is such a friend to us. Jesus has been through the very life experiences we have. Jesus does not come to us in our time of trouble just to help give us strength and courage. Jesus comes to us in our time of trouble because He has experienced the same crisis in His own time of trouble when walking this earth.

For example, in the Garden of Gethsemane Jesus asked several of his disciples to watch with him as he prayed just before his arrest. His disciples could not even do that, instead they slept. Judas Iscariot betrayed Jesus for thirty pieces of silver. Jesus was falsely accused, tried, wrongly convicted, and then put to death in the most cruel manner ever devised by man, crucifixion. Jesus came from a community with a bad reputation, Nazareth. Remember the scriptural quotation, "Can any good thing come out of Nazareth?" Jesus was misunderstood by his relatives, his friends, even his disciples.

The fact is, Jesus knows what it is like to be betrayed, falsely accused, tempted, despised and forsaken. This is the reason we can trust Jesus to be there for us when our family and friends forsake us. Jesus knows exactly how it feels to be dealt with in this manner.

A Gift From Jesus

In 1981 I met a remarkable woman named Dianne Carol McFate. My son and I had just moved back to Shreveport, Louisiana from Cut Bank, Montana. I had moved to Montana in 1979 when my natural mother became disabled in a botched suicide attempt. I had custody of my son at the time I moved to Montana. So, I took him with me so we could help my mother run her business while she recovered. I knew that, since she was disabled, she would not be likely to get a job working for anyone else. This made saving her own business to ensure her employment and livelihood critical.

Unfortunately, shortly after our arrival in Montana to help my mother, my ex-wife served me papers for another custody case. Since the court in Shreveport, Louisiana upheld its jurisdiction I was having to fight the case long distance. This meant having two lawyers, paying two legal fees, and ultimately having to return to Shreveport any number of times for court proceedings. Since there was no way I could afford these expenses I decided to move back to Shreveport. My mother finally did succeed in another suicide attempt some months after our arrival. As a result I no longer had the responsibility of helping her any further. Not only that, if I did lose custody of my son I wanted to be near enough to use whatever visitation I could get.

I set up housekeeping in Shreveport in a three-bedroom house. I had to go to work to support my son, pay bills, and try to get more money for the pending custody case. That made it clear I would need to find a reliable sitter for my son. He had met a boy down the street named Michael and spent most of his afternoons playing at his house. In the course of going down to get him for dinner I met Michael's mother, Carol. As it turned out, she was going to nursing school and worked nights to support her two children. She attended school during the day. To this day I do not know how she found the time to babysit Jeremy, but she did. Little did I know at the time the ultimate effect Carol would have in my life.

It was only a month or two after returning to Shreveport I made the mistake of taking the deposit from Burger King and running with my son so I would not lose custody. I never realized then how knowing Carol for just two months would make such a difference in my life.

As I explained in a previous chapter I did take my son and go to Seattle, Washington in the hope of keeping custody of my son. When I finally realized what a horrible mistake I had made in stealing the money to go to Seattle, I returned in the hope of making my wrong right. It occurred to me I had not only ruined my reputation in terms of getting good employment. I now would have no way of ever finding another wife who would want me. After all, I was now a convicted felon.

Once the court proceedings were out of the way I started my period of probation. I had also begun making restitution. So, I did visit Carol. I wanted her to know what had happened to me and Jeremy. After all, the night I left I did not tell anyone, not even Carol, where we were going. I was certain she was wondering what had happened to us, and I did want to see her again. The question was, once she heard what I had done and how I had now ruined my life, would she even want to talk to me? I prayed to

Jesus she would.

Carol and I did reestablish contact with each other in 1981. Still, we did not get married until 1988. I would not marry her sooner because I was having a difficult time dealing with the fact she was overweight. This may sound like a stupid attitude on my part. However, in my family looks were everything. If I dated a woman who was overweight, disabled, or not as attractive as our family had been taught a spouse should be, I was cruelly teased by the members of my family. I knew, if I married Carol, I would be exposing her to such treatment, too. It took me seven years to get up the courage to marry her despite the attitudes of my family.

If the reader has ever wondered if Jesus has a hand in choosing one's spouse, I can tell you He does. I would have never chosen Carol as a wife based on the standards set by my family. All I can say is that Jesus directed me to marry her in answer to prayers for a loving wife.

Still, I found it hard to love Carol. It was not that I did not love her. I just found it difficult to express love to her. My stepmother refusing to accept my affection had scarred me. My upbringing mentally prejudiced me against her because of her weight. More importantly, I had two previous marriages end in bitter divorces due to the ongoing custody cases with my stepmother. I was afraid Carol would divorce me the first time things got tough, too.

I prayed to Jesus to help me learn to show Carol my love. More than anything, I wanted my family to show me love. It occurred to me I had no right to ask Jesus to help my family love me if I could not show my love for Carol. I was asking Jesus to do something for me I was not willing to do for her. So, I began to pray to Jesus to help me show my love for her more.

I consider three persons in my life to be unconditional friends. One person is Jesus. The second person is my wife, Carol. I will tell you about the third person in a subsequent chapter. I know after years of bitter experiences in life these three persons will never desert me, abandon me, or despise me. Carol is without question a gift from God. The Lord knew my son would become alienated from me. The Lord knew this would devastate me. Jesus knew I needed a wife to love me and be my companion. For this reason my prayer to keep custody of my son was not answered while my prayer for a loyal friend and companion was.

The other aspect to my wife Carol which I find worth sharing with the reader is this. I wish I had not gone through the bitter experiences I have related in this book. Still, it is these very experiences which helped me learn to love her more. It is in these times of despair, pain, and hurt I learned Carol was a real friend and wife. Where my two previous wives would have been long gone due to continuing crisis, she remained by my side to love me and encourage me.

Just how wonderful a gift Carol is was evidenced by a tragedy which took place on December 18, 1996. As my wife pulled out of a post office parking lot onto a busy road an oncoming car hit her in the drivers' side door. The impact totaled our car and seriously injured my wife. The paramedics rushed her to the hospital to treat her injuries and save her life. That afternoon I got a call from a dear friend telling me what had happened. Not knowing if my wife would live or die I rushed to the hospital to be by her side.

Carol had suffered pelvic fractures and a broken hip among other injuries. It was clear she would need a long recovery period to regain her health. In the course of her long recovery she developed a life threatening surgical infection which nearly killed her. The net effect of all this was that I spent two months at home alone, without my wife. I visited her at the hospital every day with my guide dog, Frankie. Still, I also spent many lonely nights at home wondering when I would again have the company of my wonderful wife.

We often wonder why the Lord allows pain and suffering to come into our lives. I am one of those Christians who believes Satan is the one who brings pain and suffering into our lives, not the Lord. Still, one wonders why the Lord allows such suffering to come against His children. I believe my wife nearly dying in a car wreck was an attempt on Satan's part to deprive me of the one friend who would remain faithful to me for life, Carol. If Satan had his way, she would have died in that car wreck, or from her surgical infection. Nevertheless, the Lord knew I still needed Carol in my life and so he spared her life. Jesus overruled Satan's plan to take away my wife before I had truly learned to love her unconditionally.

My wife spent seven months recovering from

her accident. For the first time in our married life we could spend entire days, weeks, months together. Despite being blind I could help nurse my wife back to health. Carol used to come in from work as a nurse too exhausted to spend quality time with me. Now we were spending quality time together. During her recovery period I learned to express my love and caring for Carol. While the Lord was not responsible for her accident and injuries, He had turned something bad into something good.

Jesus had proved he was my friend again by sparing the life of my wife, Carol.

Satan Is A Liar

There is no way to describe what it is like to go blind. Whether one goes blind overnight, or goes blind over a period of many years, going blind can be a crushing experience. I can tell the reader that going blind makes one feel weak and heavy laden. The experience can leave one feeling bitter, angry and devastated for life. I have met hundreds of blind and other disabled persons who never get over their anger at the Lord for their blindness or other disability. After all, how can a loving God condemn anyone to a lifetime of blindness, deafness, paralysis, or any other disability?

Perhaps the reader is, or knows, someone who is struggling with a drug problem. Or, a friend who is an alcoholic. The same question can be asked concerning an addiction problem. How can a loving God who claims to care about us allow His children to spend their entire life struggling against an addiction, a disability, poverty or racial discrimination? If God *really* is a God of love, as the Bible says He is, surely He would intervene and spare us such hardships.

The fact is, the Lord is not the one to blame for our addictions, disabilities or other problem areas of our lives. I can best relate to being blind, because I am blind. I know as a blind person many blind people never get used to being blind. Like many blind people I have asked the Lord, "Why me?" Being blind or deaf, being an alcoholic or drug addict can leave us all asking the Lord the same question. Any of these afflictions can easily leave their victims carrying a very heavy burden in life, literally cumbered with a load of care.

How wonderful it is to know that the Lord is not the one who afflicts us or burdens us with care. He is our friend, not our tormentor. Satan wants us to believe the Lord is the one who is afflicting us because it serves his purpose for us to do so. Satan wants us to believe the Lord is a harsh taskmaster, not our friend. If Satan can succeed in making us believe the Lord does not care about us or love us, he triumphs. The reason he triumphs is because many believe the Lord is the one afflicting us. Those who believe Jesus is the one afflicting them will not trust the Lord to be a friend and help in time of need.

Satan desperately wants to separate all of us from our best friend and only hope, Jesus.

    Knowing Satan is responsible for all our griefs and afflictions is important. I am not blind because the Lord made me blind. I am blind because I live in a sinful world. A world ruled by a fallen angel whose sole joy in life is to hurt those who were created in the image of God by His son, Jesus. When Satan afflicted me with blindness he did not only cause me pain, he wounded the heart of Jesus because I am Jesus' brother, a child of the Father. Satan afflicted me with blindness hoping to so discourage me I would no longer trust Jesus as my friend. Moreover, Satan thinks when he disables us with physical disabilities and addictions he prevents us from being used by Jesus to spread the Good News. Satan believes, if he makes us the victim of racial discrimination, we will become bitter. Then, Satan hopes Jesus will not be able to use us to spread the tidings that Jesus died for our sins. Satan is convinced, if he can get us to commit crimes, our lives will be wasted away in a prison cell where we can do nothing to help tell others about Jesus. Or, be so scorned by the community upon our release from prison, no one, not even our fellow Christians, will want us in their communities or churches.

I am here to tell the reader the best news anyone could ever hope to hear. Jesus is our friend no matter what happens to us. No one can fall so low, be so weak, that Jesus cannot save them or give them a new heart. "And he said unto me, My grace is sufficient for thee; for my strength is made perfect in weakness." 2 Corinthians 12:9. In other words, when we take our weaknesses to the Lord he is able to prove how strong his ability to save is.

This text of scripture has an even more profound meaning. This scripture is telling us the worse our offenses, the greater our problems, the stronger we prove the Lord to be. You see, all Heaven is watching the battle between the Lord Jesus and Satan. Satan wants everyone to think Jesus cannot save the sinner. Even many Christians who believe Jesus can save sinners set limits on Jesus' ability to save and redeem. I cannot tell you how many times I have heard Christians state that not even Jesus can save certain people. This statement is usually made concerning persons who have committed criminal acts and have gone to prison. I must admit some crimes are so horrendous as to test even the ability of our Lord to save the person who committed them. We all wonder how Jesus can save Susan Smith for murdering her two little boys. I have heard Christians comment there is no way Jeffrey Dahmer could possibly be saved. Still, Jesus died for everyone no matter how vile their life. No matter how heinous their crime, their addiction, Jesus died for all of us. I am not going to be so presumptuous as to suggest there is anyone Jesus cannot save. The reader should not either.

You see, dear reader, here is the problem we have as sinful humans. We cannot understand how Jesus can save people who have committed such horrible crimes. Satan has spent his entire sojourn on earth perpetrating the lie that not even Jesus can save people like Jeffrey Dahmer or Susan Smith. Or, on a more fundamental level, a sinner like me or you. Unfortunately, many people who have let go of the Lord and committed horrible crimes or sins come to believe this lie. Many will go to their graves never asking for Jesus to save them because they have come to believe Jesus can save others, but not them. Nevertheless, if Susan Smith has confessed her sin to the Lord and asked for His forgiveness and salvation she will be in Heaven. Remember what the Bible says in 2 Corinthians 12:9, "... My grace is sufficient for thee; for my strength is made perfect in weakness". When did Susan Smith murder her children? In her weakness. When did Jeffrey Dahmer commit his heinous and unspeakable crimes? In his weakness. When have we committed our sins? In our weakness.

Christians love to recount the beautiful story of how Jesus, even in His dying agony, was able to save one of the malefactors hanging to one side of Him on another cross. Still, when it comes to many Christians showing the same love and forgiveness toward persons who are condemned, we fail. Still, when did the thief on the cross commit his crimes? In his weakness. Nevertheless, having been brought to the end of his life as a sinner, this criminal came face to face with his only hope, Jesus. For every person who has ever questioned the sincerity of a jail house conversion I would hold up this story as proof they do occur. Such a conversion does not remove the burden of the condemned to face their punishment in this life. The malefactor on the cross next to Jesus still had to pay the price for his crimes and face his death on the cross. Did this fact keep Jesus from saving him? According to Luke 23:43 Jesus was just as able to save this sinner as they both hung on a cross as when he ministered in towns and villages. "And Jesus said unto him; Verily I say unto thee, To day shalt thou be with me in paradise."

    This scripture sounds clear to me, Jesus saved the thief on the cross despite society putting him to death. This example should be a lesson to every Christian. While criminals have to face the penalty for their crimes, we must extend the love of Jesus to them, and to every other soul languishing in sin.

    The point is, Jesus is a friend to everyone. He did not die just for Christians who were leading exemplary lives. He did not shed His saving blood for people who were deserving in their own right. Jesus died for every soul who would call upon Him and claim His saving grace. The thief on the cross was a malefactor whom the government had sentenced to death. In our society, he would have to be considered a felony offender of a capital crime to get the death penalty. So, the thief on the cross was no petty criminal. This man had engaged in some serious criminal activity. Still, this hurting, lost soul did not believe the lie of Satan that God could not love and save him. This man saw in Jesus his only hope of salvation. As the scripture I quoted in the previous paragraph shows, Jesus was quick to extend salvation to this repentant soul.

Unfortunately, the malefactor who hung on the other side of Jesus did believe Satan's lie. This unfortunate criminal, this lost soul, chose to believe the lie that God could not love him because he had fallen too low in sin. Instead of joining the other thief in asking for saving grace this thief died in his sins convinced nothing could save him.

I cannot tell you how many times I have told myself there was simply no way Jesus would want to save someone as wretched as me. I stole the money from Burger King, I had my chest tattooed, I have denied Jesus on many occasions. Yet, Jesus has always let me know there is no one He cannot save. Indeed, I have come to realize I should never be presumptuous enough to suppose there is anyone Jesus cannot save, myself included. To deny the power of Jesus to save whomever He chooses is to deny His sacrifice on Calvary. Once we realize this profound truth, there is no way Satan can deceive us with the lie that we are too fallen for Jesus to save us. Church members may abandon us as unworthy of their fellowship. Christian family members may forsake us as unworthy to love or nurture in the love of Jesus. Still, dear friend, Jesus will be there to help carry our heavy load and give us help in dealing with our cares.

Understanding Jesus does not force His friendship upon us is important for the reader. It is our decision to invite Jesus into our hearts. It is up to us to ask Jesus to forgive us our sins. The good news is the Holy Spirit comes to us to help encourage us to come to Jesus and lay our burdens at His feet. The Holy Spirit does not force himself upon us either. Still, when we are in sin, the Holy Spirit comes to us and woos us back to Jesus. All we need do is answer the call of the Holy Spirit and ask Jesus to forgive us and help us and He will. The fact is it was the Holy Spirit working on the hearts of the two malefactors hanging on either side of Jesus that day on Calvary. Still, it was up to the two men to decide how they would respond to the pleadings of the Holy Spirit. As we know, one accepted

Jesus and asked Jesus to remember him. The other malefactor rejected the pleadings of the Holy Spirit.

As I have said earlier in this book, this is the reason I am citing my own experiences in this book. It is in these experiences I came to know Jesus was my friend and loved me. I always knew He loved me, I think deep down inside we all do. Still, it was in the experiences I related in this book where I learned something of the depth and breadth of the love of Jesus. Reading inspirational accounts of how Jesus saved a thief on the cross tells us of the love of Jesus. Finding out how much Jesus loves us as we encounter bitter life experiences speaks to us personally.

Friend, I do not care where this book finds you, Jesus through His Holy Spirit is by your side this very moment. Are you in a prison cell with no hope of release because of the heinous nature of your crime? Are you in prison because someone has falsely accused you and you were not able to prove your innocence? Are you sitting home alone sobbing your heart out because a beloved child, loved one, friend, or dear spouse has died? Friend, Jesus is right there beside you now waiting to hear your prayer for hope, love and friendship. There is no burden, no care so great Jesus cannot help you survive the pain. He will not bring back your deceased spouse, but He can reunite you both in the Resurrection. He may not help you get free of your prison cell in this life. However, He cannot be kept from you by any prison cell no matter how well fortified or secluded. Jesus may not help you prove your innocence when you are falsely accused. Yet, Jesus can use the experience to help you learn to trust His love and friendship.

Let me give you an example of why our burdens and cares can work together for our good. I would never have written this book except for the bitter experiences I have gone through in my life. I know this book is going to inspire thousands of people to ask Jesus to come into their hearts as they encounter the trials of life. Hurting souls will learn there is no situation in which Jesus cannot help. Knowing this makes all the bitter experiences I have lived through a blessing. Satan is defeated by this witness.

Again, Jesus did not inflict these bitter experiences on me so I would have material for this book. Satan inflicted these bitter experiences on me so I would be so devastated I could never witness to anyone about the love of Jesus. How wonderful it is that Jesus can take such a diabolical plan of Satan and turn it to His glory to benefit others.

Perhaps your bitter experiences, your trials have left you so devastated you cannot imagine being able ever to witness for the Lord either. Dear friend, it is because of the bitterness of the experience, the utter devastation of the trial you are passing through that makes your situation so powerful a testimony about Jesus. Do not give Satan the victory by cursing God or giving up as too unworthy to have a friend like Jesus. Instead, defeat the purpose of Satan and let Jesus come to your defense. Let the world see how Jesus loves and works to save the downtrodden, the rejected, the devastated.

A Real Friend In Jesus

Every time I hear, or sing, my favorite gospel hymn, "What A Friend We Have In Jesus" I think of a friend, Hubert Hunt.
This book is about what a friend we have in Jesus. Still, Jesus knows how important it is for us to have true friends in the flesh too. We are blessed if we only find one true friend in our entire life. For me one of my truest friends is Hubert Hunt. I am convinced his friendship is a gift from God. The reason I am including an account of my friendship with Hubert in this book is because Hubert more closely reflects the love and friendship of Jesus than any other person I know on earth. I hope talking about how wonderful a friend he has been in this book inspires some reader to be that kind of friend to someone else. If it does, then this chapter has served its purpose to foster the love of Jesus.
The key to my friendship with Hubert has always been, in my opinion, the fact we know we are both human. In other words, we both know neither one of us is perfect. He has made his

share of mistakes in dealing with me. And, I have made my share of mistakes in dealing with Hubert. Still, whatever hurt or problems we have caused each other in life, we always remain friends. Our friendship is not based on whether we have ever made mistakes or not. You see. The problem with most friendships is this. As long as our friends do exactly what we think they should, we will be their loyal friend. However, let them make a mistake or cause us some hurt and that is the end of the friendship. This is what leads parents to disown children, husbands and wives to get divorced despite their solemn vow to God to stay married "til death do us part." Someone in the relationship falls short of the others expectations, end of friendship.

This is what makes my friendship with Hubert so valuable. He does me wrong, we remain friends. I do some wrong to Him, we remain friends. During the course of our friendship we have both been able to help the other through some tough times. Still, had we ever parted company as friends due to some grudge or misunderstanding we would not have been able to help each other out in hard times.

In the course of my friendship with Hubert, I

committed the Burger King theft I related in the first chapter. Hubert could have walked away at the time not wanting to be associated with a man who was a convicted criminal. Nevertheless, Hubert showed the love of Jesus to me by remaining my friend. When I was falsely accused of molesting children, Hubert could have said he did not want a friend accused of such a heinous crime. Hubert continued to reflect the love of Jesus in his heart by remaining my loyal friend. Yet, other Christian friends deserted me. The church I attended at that time disfellowshipped me and asked me never to return.

When I became blind, my own family ignored my blindness. They have never, to this day, uttered one word of sympathy or love concerning my blindness. Hubert could have treated me the same way because many people do not want the hassle of a blind or disabled friend. Once again, Hubert has showed the love of Jesus by encouraging me in my blindness where others did not. Hubert has proven himself to be the kind of friend Jesus is. Can you imagine what the world would be like if everyone reflected the love and character of Jesus like Hubert does?

Keep in mind, Hubert is not a minister or

missionary in the formal sense of the word. Hubert works for a living like every other person has to do. Hubert would be the first to admit he is an ordinary mortal with failings just like the rest of us. Still, Hubert is a minister in that he has shown me more Christian love and encouragement to others than many ministers have. Why? Because, whether Hubert realizes it or not, he reflects the love of Jesus.

Hubert has a friend who has spent over twenty years in prison. This friend confessed to a crime which was apparently committed by the man's girlfriend. Being a macho type of guy Hubert's friend was not going to let a woman take the rap for any crime. In this case, the murder of a police officer. Whether it was the girlfriend who killed the officer, or Hubert's friend, it was Hubert's friend who got life in prison.

Most people abandoned this man completely. Who wants to be the friend of a convicted murderer? More than that, who wants to spend their valuable time visiting this man in prison on weekends? Or take valuable time to write him letters of encouragement? Or, send him items he might need while in prison? No one I know of, except the man's sister, and Hubert. Does the fact Hubert continues to be his friend mean Hubert condones what the friend did? Of course not. Jesus is our friend even though He does not condone our sins. The point is Hubert knows this man is his brother in Christ and treats him accordingly. Hubert also knows, as we all should, but, for the grace of God, it could be him, me, or the reader in that prison cell.

I hope the Lord will bless Hubert with a long life on this earth. He is the kind of friend we all should have the privilege of knowing. Hubert is not blest with wealth. Hubert has had enough hardships and crisis in his own life. He could easily excuse his need to do anything for anyone else. Amazingly, Hubert has done everything he has for his friends out of his own need, not out of any surplus he had at the time.

I remember in 1987 when I had been living with my brother for about six months in Dallas, Texas. I was having a real rough time of it and could not afford rent or groceries. So, I had asked my brother to put me up for some months until I could get back on my feet. My brother did so. One day my brother decided to move back to our parents home because he wanted to relocate.

For his relocation to be possible he was going to have to stay with my parents for awhile until he could find a place to live and get a job. My brother's move would leave me without a place to live. This meant I would need to move, too. Except, I had no other place to move to.

When the day of the move came, I helped my brother load his U-Haul and we made the 180 mile trip from Dallas to Waskom, Texas. I asked him if he had explained to our stepmother I would need to spend a few days in her home too until I could find a place to stay. He assured me he had discussed it with my stepmother and she had said it would be alright. Confident he really had talked it over with her I did not bring up the subject again. We made a second trip back to Dallas to get the rest of his belongings. By the time we returned to our parents house to have dinner and relax we were both exhausted.

Since we had been skirting severe thunderstorms and tornadoes we were also glad to get off the road and inside shelter. The minute we walked inside the house my stepmother wanted to know why I was still with my brother. I explained it was my understanding she and my father had agreed to let me stay there two or three days. This would allow me the time to get a place to stay.

My stepmother let me know no such agreement had been reached with my brother on my behalf. Knowing my stepmother was a devout Christian I hoped she would change her mind. Amazingly, my stepmother did not change her mind. She ordered me out of the house at once without so much as even offering me dinner. The television news had just announced a tornado was in the area so I was hesitant to go outside and sleep in my car. Still, she offered me no alternative and I had no money for a motel. Moreover, no one, not even my brother would come to my rescue and try to talk her into letting me stay the night. In fact, it was clear from my stepmothers remarks my brother had known I was not going to be welcome once we got there. He just did not want to jeopardize his moving help.

I went outside and spent the night in my car. All that night I was buffeted by severe winds, rain, hail and the fear a tornado would hit while I was without adequate shelter. The next morning I went over to see my friend, Hubert. It was my hope he would be more merciful to me than my family had been. I explained my situation to Hubert and asked if he would be kind enough to put me up for a few weeks until I could get a job and some rent money. Remember, dear reader, Hubert did not make a lot of money and was in less of a position to help me than my family was. What did Hubert do? He offered me the hospitality of his home for however long I needed it. Then he did something even more astounding.

Due to the fact Hubert lived alone he only had one bedroom of his mobile home furnished. I had already told Hubert I would be happy to sleep on the floor. However, that would not do for Hubert. He went out and bought a complete bed set so I would be able to sleep comfortably. Noticing I needed a pair of new shoes, he went to the store with me and bought me a pair of new shoes. When I could not find a job and enrolled in a vocational school a week later he loaned me the money to buy the tools I would need to train with.

The point of me relating this situation to you is not to slander my family in how they treated me in this matter. Rather, what I am trying to do is show the contrast between how my stepmother, a devout Christian, and Hubert, also a Christian, treated someone in need. Hubert is the one who accurately reflected the love of Jesus. Hubert is the one whose friendship is what I consider to be a type for the friendship of Jesus. Hubert helped me out of his sense of what Jesus would do in a similar situation, not out of any financial surplus.

I could go on to tell the reader story after story of how Hubert has helped others in the same situation. Of how Hubert has donated tens of thousands of dollars to church ministries and persons in need of help. Of how he has extended his compassion and friendship to some of the very people other Christians would be loathe to help. Hubert always comes down on the side Jesus would, and that is a good side to be on.

In closing this chapter on Hubert, I want to remind the reader Hubert is not, and does not claim to be a perfect Christian. He has made serious mistakes in his Christian experience, just like we all have. Still, Hubert has never chosen to believe the lie of Satan that Jesus cannot love those who make mistakes or fall short of the calling of God in the flesh.

My friendship with Hubert reminds me of a

scripture which aptly describes what a friend he is. It goes like this, "....and there is a friend that sticketh closer than a brother". Proverbs 18:24.

    Let us all strive to be the kind of friend to others that Jesus is. Let us all work to be the kind of friend to others that Hubert Hunt is. In doing so, we will win more lost souls to Jesus than all the preaching and bible study ever will. I know there are those who read this book who will disagree with the statement I am about to make. Still, it is a statement which needs to be made. Christians of all denominations have fallen woefully short of showing the love of Jesus to others less fortunate than themselves. Moreover, many Christians have fallen woefully short of being the kind of friend to others Jesus expects us to be. So let me close this chapter with another scripture which I think says it all. "Beloved, let us love one another: for love is of God; and every one that loveth is born of God, and knoweth God. I John 4:7-8, "In this was manifested the love of God toward us, because that God sent his only begotten Son into the world that we might live through him. Herein is love, not that we loved God, but that he loved us, and sent his Son to be the propitiation for our sins. Beloved, if God so loved us, we ought also to love one another". I John 4:9-11.

Just As We Are

There will be many who read this book who have a sound relationship with Jesus. For the reader who has an ongoing relationship with Jesus this chapter may not mean much. Still, many who read this book have forgotten about what a friend Jesus is, or perhaps never knew at all. There will be many readers who feel so unworthy they will be ashamed to call upon the Lord to be their friend. I can recall many occasions when I felt so ashamed of my life I was literally embarrassed to call upon the name of the Lord. This chapter will be like a nugget of pure gold to the reader who needs to have Jesus as their friend.

First, dear brother or sister, realize Jesus wants you to come to him just as you are right now. Do not think for a moment he will not accept you as you are. I know of many times when I have committed some sin I would realize I had done wrong and would want to immediately pray to Jesus for forgiveness. Satan would then discourage me by telling me I was not fit to go to Jesus in prayer and ask for his forgiveness. After all, had I not committed the sin willingly? Friend, this is a lie of the highest order. Do not let Satan deceive you into beleiving Jesus has deserted you. Or, that some sin you have committed has made you unfit to go back to Jesus. "For when we were still without strength, in due time Christ died for the ungodly. For scarcely for a righteous man will one die; yet perhaps for a good man someone would even dare to die. But God demonstrates His own love toward us, in that while we were yet sinners, Christ died for us." Romans 5:6-8.

This text makes it clear. Jesus died for us while we were yet sinners. How much clearer can it be, dear friend? Jesus wants sinners to come to him and ask for his salvation and help *just as we are.* Only Satan does not want the sinner to come to Jesus or fellowship with other believers.

Despite this text, I still have men and women who have fallen so low, who have hated God so much, they are certain even this text does not apply to them. Some of these dear men and women have told me they were not just sinners, they were enemies of God. Surely, they tell me,

God cannot extend His love and grace to His avowed enemies. This is still another lie promoted by Satan to keep lost souls in need of Jesus' love from asking for it. "For if when we were enemies we were reconciled to God through the death of His Son, much more, having been reconciled, we shall be saved by His life." Romans 5:10.

How much clearer could it be, dear friend. Jesus has reconciled us to God while we were still His enemies. So, there is no one who cannot ask for, and freely receive, the friendship and forgiveness of Jesus. "For by grace you have been saved through faith, and that not of yourselves; it is the gift of God." Ephesians 2:8.

Friend, no matter where you are in your life right now, ask Jesus to be your friend and He will. Do not let your present circumstances prevent you from asking Jesus to be your friend. You may be in a hospital bed, a disability rehab center, a youth offender bootcamp, or be sitting in a prison cell for some crime you have, or have not committed. It does not matter. Ask Jesus to be your friend right now, this moment. "Let us therefore come boldly to the throne of grace, that we may obtain mercy and find grace to help in the time of need." Hebrews 4:16. Do what this text says to do. Go to Jesus boldly and ask Him for mercy. Let Jesus give you the grace you need in your time of need and He will. Do not believe the lie of Satan that Jesus will not hear or help you due to your sins or failures.

"And it shall come to pass that whoever calls on the name of the Lord shall be saved." Acts 2:21. How much easier could Jesus make it, dear friend? All we have to do is call upon His name and we are saved. Jesus is our friend. "But when the wicked turns from his wickedness and does what is lawful and right, he shall live because of it." Ezekiel 33:19.

Once you have called upon Jesus to be your friend, believe he is your friend. Abide in His love and friendship. Trust Jesus to be a true and faithful friend to you. Do not judge the love of Jesus by how others treat you. Do not let the way other Christians treat you determine how you will temper your relationship with Jesus. As I have pointed out many times in this book I was often the most scorned by fellow Christians. The very people who should have been the most loving to me in my hour of trial and need. Jesus does not deal with us in this manner. So, do not let how other humans treat you determine whether or not you have a relationship with Jesus.

Once you have gone to Jesus and asked for His friendship and love, what do you do next? Begin to reflect the love Jesus has graced you with to others. "Beloved, if God so loved us, we also ought to love one another." I John 4:11. This is the whole gospel in a nutshell. We are to do for others what Jesus has done for us. His life and ministry on earth, his horrible crucifixion to provide us salvation, all this Jesus has done for us out of unconditional love.

By showing this same love to those we deal with everyday we are reflecting the character of Jesus. We are offering hope and peace to others, who like us, may be desperate for a true friend.

Finally, dear brother or sister, live at peace with yourself. "You will keep him in perfect peace, whose mind is stayed on You, because he trusts in You. Isaiah 26:3. Put your confidence in Jesus. If you fall again, Jesus will be there to pick you up. Should you fall into some sin you were certain you had overcome, take it to the Lord in prayer. Jesus will not leave your side just because you make mistakes. Never again believe the lie of Satan that you cannot go to Jesus after you have made another mistake.

To those readers who are Christians and have a relationship with Jesus, remember, He has given you a gift of grace. Do not be like the Pharisee's of Jesus day and stand on the corner to proclaim your own goodness. Share the grace and friendship Jesus has offered you to everyone you meet irregardless of their station in life. It is a disgrace to the name of Jesus when Christians refuse to show the love of Jesus to others in need of it. When Christians do not extend the love of Jesus to the downtrodden Satan triumphs.

Jesus never turned his back on anyone in need of love and friendship. From the prostitute, Mary Magdalene, to the condemned thief on the cross, Jesus never denied His grace and love to anyone. As Christians we should not either.

I would also recommend to every brother and sister reading this book to find other Christians to fellowship with. This is the death blow to Satan and his lies. If you begin to fellowship with the friends of Jesus, whatever their denomination, Satan loses his power over you.

If you begin to fellowship with a group of Christians who do not want a sinner in their fellowship depart from them. These people have forgotten they are sinners too and as dependent on Jesus' grace as you are. The love of Jesus is not in such a group. It does not matter how fancy their sanctuary or holy sounding their church name is. Unless they share the love of Jesus with you, Jesus does not abide with them.

Whatever your past experience with unloving churches, never give up. If you are in prison search out the Chaplain and begin to fellowship with other Christians in prison. If there is nothing preventing you from searching out a loving church in the community, then, keep searching until you find one. I can tell you from personal experience the Holy Spirit will guide you where he wants you to go.

In my own case, I was led to a very loving church called Westminster Presbyterian Church in Casselberry, Florida. The purpose of this book is not to promote any denomination or doctrinal system. My point in mentioning this church is simply to illustrate there are loving churches in the community which do show the love of Jesus to others.

I recall the first day I attended Westminster Presbyterian Church. My wife read me the sign out front as we drove into the parking lot. The sign simply stated, "All Are Welcome Here". Words are cheap and I was anxious to see if this statement was true, or just a fancy phrase that looked good out front on the church sign. I learned over the years the congregation lived by that statement.

Whatever your denominational preference, go to church so you can fellowship with other friends of Jesus. This is something Satan will work desperately to prevent you from doing. He knows if you fellowship with other friends of Jesus he has lost the battle for your soul. Do not forsake the fellowship of other real Christians who understand Jesus is a friend to all. Do not let Satan have the victory in your life.

"Trust in the Lord with all your heart, and lean not on your own understanding; in all your ways acknowledge Him, and He shall direct your paths". Proverbs 3:5-6.

About The Author

Harry Martin is a 100% service connected, disabled veteran. Mr. Martin became totally blind as the result of an eye disease he contracted while serving in the Navy. In addition to this book he has written an educational resource book titled, "What Blind People Wish Sighted People Knew About Blindness".

Harry and his wife, Carol, attend the Westminister Presbyterian Church in Casselberry, Florida. Mr. Martin is an avid bowler on the Westminster Church Bowling League. He also enjoys backpacking, canoeing, and woodworking.

Mr. Martin is available to speak to church groups on the subject of this book for a love offering to help defray expenses.

*

How To Order Additional Copies:

To order copies of this book send $9.95 and $2.00 shipping and handling per copy to:

Harry Martin, Author
2314 River Park Circle, #2111
Orlando, FL 32817-4828

* Please make checks payable to Harry Martin.

Church groups ordering this book in quantities of fifty copies or more may purchase it for $5.95 & $1.00 S&H per copy.

Prison ministries may purchase *single* copies of this book for $5.95 & $1.00 S&H. Please supply complete mailing address and name of Chaplain making the request. When ordered in quantities of ten or more prison ministries may purchase this book for $5.00 & $1.00 S&H a copy.

Special Note: One dollar of the purchase price of this book is contributed to the Love Offering of the Westminister Presbyterian Church in Casselberry, Florida.

If this book has made a difference in your life and been a blessing to you, please write the Author at the address above and let him know. The Author would love to hear how this book has helped the reader. You may also reach the Author at HMartin740@aol.com or HarryMartin1@compuserve.com. Fax: 407-207-3185.

A MUST READ FOR SIGHTED PEOPLE!

A MUST LISTEN FOR THE BLIND!

190 pages, softcover, $14.95 & $3 S&H per copy.
http://www.light-communications.com/author/martin/sighted.htm

Send Check or M.O. to:
Harry Martin, Author
2314 River Park Circle, #2111
Orlando, Florida, USA 32817-4828